Most snakes look after their eggs.

Fish lay eggs.

What Lays Eggs?

Many animals lay eggs.

Snakes lay eggs.

Most fish do not look after their eggs.

Snails lay eggs.

Snails do not look after
their eggs.

Mosquitoes lay eggs.

Mosquitoes do not look after their eggs.

Chickens lay eggs, too!

Chickens look after
their eggs.

Inside an Egg

7 DAYS OLD

18 DAYS OLD

20 DAYS OLD

HATCHING TIME!

Index

chickens   12–15

fish   6–7

mosquitoes   10–11

snails   8–9

snakes   4–5

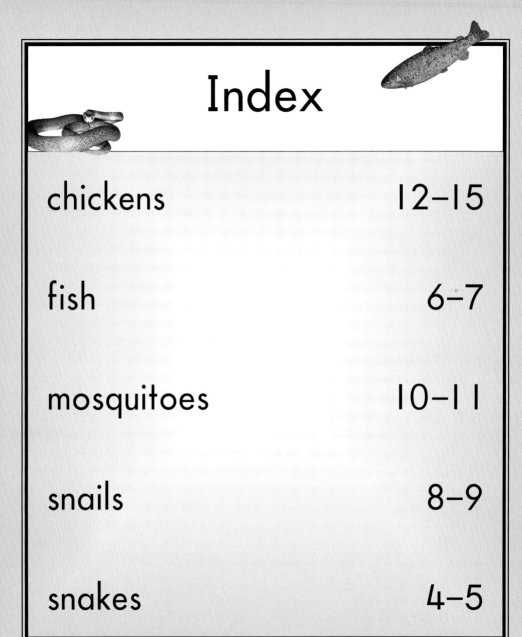